Nocturnal
Animals

Owls

by Mary R. Dunn

Consulting Editor: Gail Saunders-Smith, PhD

Consultant: Tanya Dewey, PhD
University of Michigan Museum of Zoology

Pebble Plus is published by Capstone Press,
1710 Roe Crest Drive, North Mankato, Minnesota 56003.
www.capstonepub.com

Books published by Capstone Press are manufactured with paper
containing at least 10 percent post-consumer waste.

Library of Congress Cataloging-in-Publication Data
Dunn, Mary R.
Owls / by Mary Dunn.
   p. cm.—(Pebble plus. Nocturnal animals)
   Includes bibliographical references and index.
   Summary: "Simple text and full-color photos explain the habitat, life cycle, range, and behavior of owls"—Provided
by publisher.
   ISBN 978-1-4296-5997-0 (library binding)
   ISBN: 978-1-4296-7119-4 (paperback)
 1. Owls—Juvenile literature. I. Title. II. Series.
QL696.S8D865 2012
598.9'7—dc22   2011001052

Editorial Credits
Lori Shores, editor; Gene Bentdahl, designer; Wanda Winch, media researcher; Laura Manthe, production specialist

Photo Credits
Alamy: FLPA/Mike Jones, 17, Juniors Bildarchiv, 21, Nick Ball, 1, Photoshot Holdings Ltd, 5, 13, Rick & Nora Bowers,
7, Rolf Nussbaumer Photography, 19; Shutterstock: mlorenz, 9, P. Schwarz, 11; SuperStock: All Canada Photos, cover,
Barry Mansell, 15

Note to Parents and Teachers

The Nocturnal Animals series supports national science standards related to life science.
This book describes and illustrates owls. The images support early readers in understanding the
text. The repetition of words and phrases helps early readers learn new words. This book also
introduces early readers to subject-specific vocabulary words, which are defined in the Glossary
section. Early readers may need assistance to read some words and to use the Table
of Contents, Glossary, Read More, Internet Sites, and Index sections of the book.

Printed in the United States of America in North Mankato, Minnesota.
062012   006762R

Table of Contents

Night Hunters

Most owls sleep all day.

These nocturnal birds

wing their way through

the night sky.

About 200 kinds of owls
live around the world.
They make their homes
in other birds' nests
or holes in trees.

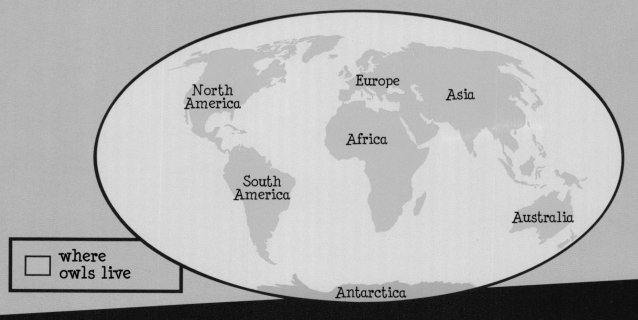

North
America

Europe

Asia

Africa

South
America

Australia

Antarctica

where
owls live

Up Close!

Owls come in all sizes.

Some owls weigh up to

9 pounds (4 kilograms).

Other owls weigh

less than 1 pound (.45 kg).

Owls have gray-white or brown-orange feathers. Soft wing feathers help owls fly silently.

Finding Food

Big eyes and keen ears
help owls find prey.
They use sharp talons
to grab mice, lizards,
and birds.

Owls gulp small prey
in one bite.
They use sharp beaks
to tear apart large prey.

Growing Up

Female owls lay
round, white eggs.
Chicks hatch from the eggs
in about 30 days.

Male owls feed chicks

many times each day.

The young owls are

strong enough to fly

in five to seven weeks.

Staying Safe

Large birds and cats eat owls.

Owls always listen for danger.

Owls that stay safe can live

more than 20 years.

Glossary

beak—the hard front part of the mouth of birds; also called a bill

hatch—to break out of an egg

keen—able to notice things easily

nest—a home built by an animal

nocturnal—active at night and resting during the day

prey—an animal hunted by another animal for food

talon—a long, sharp claw

Read More

Mattern, Joanne. *The Pebble First Guide to Nocturnal Animals.* Pebble First Guides. Mankato, Minn.: Capstone Press, 2010.

Patrick, Roman. *Snowy Owls.* Animals That Live in the Tundra. New York: Gareth Stevens Pub., 2011.

Thomson, Ruth. *The Life Cycle of an Owl.* Learning about Life Cycles. New York: Rosen Pub. Group/PowerKids Press, 2009.

Internet Sites

FactHound offers a safe, fun way to find Internet sites related to this book. All of the sites on FactHound have been researched by our staff.

Here's all you do:

Visit *www.facthound.com*

Type in this code: 9781429659970

Check out projects, games and lots more at
www.capstonekids.com

Index

Word Count: 164

Grade: 1

Early-Intervention Level: 13